Winter Recipes
Angela Gray's Cookery School
Published in Great Britain in 2016 by
Graffeg Limited

Written by Angela Gray copyright © 2016.
Food photography by Huw Jones
copyright © 2016.
Food styling by André Moore.
Designed and produced by Graffeg Limited
copyright © 2016

Graffeg Limited, 24 Stradey Park Business
Centre, Mwrwg Road, Llangennech,
Llanelli, Carmarthenshire SA14 8YP Wales
UK Tel 01554 824000 www.graffeg.com

Angela Gray is hereby identified as the
authors of this work in accordance with
section 77 of the Copyrights, Designs and
Patents Act 1988.

A CIP Catalogue record for this book is
available from the British Library.

ISBN 9781910862674

1 2 3 4 5 6 7 8 9

Photo credits

Pages 6-147 © Huw Jones

Page 150-151 © Harry Williams
Photography

Pages 148, 152, 153, 154, 156
© A L S Photography
www.alsphotography.co.uk

Angela Gray's
Cookery School
Winter Recipes

Photographs Huw Jones

GRAFFEG

Contents

Desserts

Introduction

Welcome to my winter kitchen. This is the first in a series of books celebrating the seasons and the wonderful and varied ingredients they bring. For me, winter is a time of year when we tend to do more cooking and entertaining.

The warmth of the kitchen and the creative space there beckons us to cook, to conjure up comforting food to nurture ourselves and others. Cooking and eating can really lift the spirits, feeding both body and soul, and this collection of recipes is designed to do just that.

I have used classic combinations of ingredients to add complexity to the recipes. From vibrant aromatic spice blends such as Arabic "*Baharat*" and north African Ras el hanout, to the punchy flavours of citrus, porcini and pomegranate molasses.

These ingredients and more have influenced a wide range of dishes from barbecued hot smoked salmon and seafood masala, to the lengthier slow-cooked Game Tagine and Osso Bucco. Winter puddings are like a big hug – very important - so I have included a few of my favourites, which won't disappoint!

The recipes reflect treasured memories of my childhood, my travels and culinary adventures, the many places I have worked and the influential food writers and chefs that have helped me shape my craft. They have been tried and tested over the years and have proved to be both practical and very successful in my School at Llanerch Vineyard.

From a very young age I have had a fascination with food. For instance, I remember being taken to a Chinese restaurant when I was 5 years old. As we approached I detected an aroma diffusing into the night air, I tried to work out what it was, but it was totally alien to me, but very exciting. I had to know more and was desperate to taste something and was rewarded with my first prawn cracker!

Well, I've come a long way since then, but it was the inquisitiveness and quest to learn, to experiment and taste that led to an exciting and really fulfilling career in food. My teachers have been many; starting with the Galloping Gourmet, who probably was the first exciting, high-energy chef on television. He flambéed everything and the food looked amazing, such a contrast to what we were eating

in those days. He would grab someone from the audience to eat with him and by then I would be on all fours sniffing the television! I swear I could smell the food!

My mum's *Cordon Bleu* magazines in the 60s had pictures of food I had never seen before. She cooked some of the recipes and I would be at her side savouring the rich, complex and seductive aromas. Later on the Roux brothers' books became an important influence, their exacting and classic approach to food helped me refine and develop my own skill base. Then there were the wonderful food writers: Jane Grigson, Elizabeth David, Claudia Roden and even Mrs. Beeton were all with me growing up in my foodie world. The layering of skills and culinary styles coupled with a zest for life and meeting people led me on to my dream job.

Teaching people to cook is such an honour; those who have been in my classes will know that I have a lot to say! I want to share what I have learned over the years and am passionate about empowering people to challenge their potential in the kitchen and grow their culinary confidence. It's really wonderful when you witness an awakening in someone, as I have many times. It could be from simply roasting and blending spices, which is always an amazing start to a class, or mastering knife skills and preparing a range of fish, or baking something spectacular from just a few ingredients – it's magical and so satisfying. They realise the possibilities are endless and leave inspired.

My approach to cooking is a little Zen-like. I describe it as culinary meditation, where you can totally focus on the job in hand, relax yourself into the process of preparing all the ingredients and expand your mind whilst you are creating the dish. You can see possibilities within what you are doing and apply them to your everyday cooking. It's so relaxing and, of course, the experience goes on as you then have the enjoyment of eating and sharing the food you have made.

The recipes that follow echo all of this. I describe them as entertainment for the pallet, like a firework that starts off with a little splutter of sparkle, then erupts into ever increasing levels of energy and colour with a big finish. The result being: eyes widen, the jaw drops slightly and the "wow" factor ensues. There's a richness and opulence to many of the dishes and the colours are as deep as the flavours. Some of them can be whipped up in a short time, whilst others require longer slow cooking.

As you approach a cooking session, remember, focus only on what you are doing and enjoy the experience of preparing and cooking and ultimately of course, the eating.

Angela Gray

Winter Garden

A great sharing dish with friends and family, packed full of flavour, colour and textures. All you need is some homemade bread to scoop up all the goodies, try the gremolata bread.

Ingredients

Butternut squash Purée

400g roasted butternut squash

5 roasted cloves garlic

1 flat teaspoon sea salt

Freshly ground black pepper

2 tablespoons tahini

1 teaspoon lemon zest

1 tablespoon lemon juice

½ teaspoon fresh nutmeg

½ teaspoon cinnamon

¼ teaspoon ground cumin

Nuts and seeds

200g almonds, hazelnuts or walnuts

1 tablespoon sesame seeds

Pickled vegetables

1 large floret of cauliflower

1 large floret broccoli

1 medium carrot

4 radish

100ml white wine vinegar

1 bay leaf

6 peppercorns

½ teaspoon maple syrup

3 sprigs of dill (optional) or ½ teaspoon fennel seeds

Marinated Feta

100g feta cheese

2 tablespoons olive oil

1 small chilli (optional) sliced thinly

Peeled zest of 1 lemon cut into julienne shreds

1 tablespoon maple syrup

Sea salt and black pepper

To finish

3 sprigs of curly or flat leaf parsley

Alfalfa or sprouted beans

Serves 4

What you do

Marinated feta

This is always better done the day before. Cut the feta into mini cubes and place into a small bowl. Mix together the oil, chilli, lemon zest (boil the lemon zest in the maple syrup for 5 minutes, cool), sprinkle with cracked black pepper and pour over the feta. Cover and chill until needed – you will need to take it out of the fridge an hour before you use it.

Pickled vegetables

Prepare the florets of cauliflower and broccoli, cutting mini florets to resemble tiny plants. Cut the carrot into thin slices and cut out with a cutter to form a frilly edge. If you don't have a cutter, cut slices in half and cut a little frill edge by hand. Cut the radish into thin slices and then in half. Place all the prepared vegetables in a bowl. Heat the vinegar with the bay leaf, peppercorns and maple syrup, bring to the boil, then pour over the vegetables. Cool, cover and chill.

To make the purée

Place everything in a processor and blitz to form a smooth paste.

Taste and adjust with seasoning and lemon so you have a yummy, well-rounded flavour.

Finally, the nut soil

This need to be done fresh on the day. Dry roast the nuts in a pan until they are golden, add the sesame seeds and cook until everything is deep golden. Cool slightly and then process in a blender to create a nutty soil.

To assemble

Make sure everything is at room temperature – apart from the pickles, they can be used straight from the fridge. Divide the purée between 4 serving plates, using the back of a spoon to spread it out to create the base of your garden. Sprinkle the nut soil over to cover. Then plant your pickled vegetables, parsley leaves, alfalfa and feta cubes to create your pretty winter garden.

To serve

Serve with griddled flat bread. Utterly delicious and so good for you!

Mixed Grain Pilaf with Roasted Leeks and Preserved Lemon

I love this dish. When I come home after a busy day, I love to unwind with the preparation and cooking of this recipe. It's a bowl full of good, wholesome energy and is also great as a salad.

Ingredients

2 tablespoons rapeseed or olive oil

1 small onion, peeled and finely chopped

1 large leek, trimmed and shredded

1 fat clove garlic, finely grated with a little sea salt

100g freekeh

100g bulgur wheat

100g red carmargue rice

Approximately 450ml good flavoured vegetable stock

3 whole large leaves kale, shredded

1 large stick celery, peeled and sliced

To finish

3 sprigs mint, leaves chopped

6 sprigs parsley, stalks chopped finely, leaves roughly chopped

A handful of seedless grapes, halved

100g feta, drained and crumbled

Dressing

1 fat garlic clove, finely grated with a little sea salt

1 preserved lemon, pips removed and finely chopped

6 tablespoons olive oil

1 teaspoon tahini paste

A little agave or maple syrup to balance the flavour

Serves 4

What you do

1 First, check the packet instructions on your grains (freekeh, bulgur wheat and rice) for the cooking times, they do vary. Then you are set to start with the one that takes the longest, gradually adding them to the pilaf so they are all ready at the same time.

2 To make the pilaf, use a large pan and add the oil over a medium heat, add the onion, stir through then add

a couple of tablespoons of stock to help speed up the softening process. Once they are soft, turn up the heat and add the leeks, stir-fry until softened and lightly golden.

③ Add the garlic then stir in the grains, cover with vegetables stock, pop on a lid and simmer gently over a low heat until the grains are cooked. You may need to add a little more stock during cooking to ensure they are thoroughly cooked through.

④ Use a fork to rake the grains so they separate, stir in the kale and celery. Remove from the heat and mix in the herbs, grapes and feta.

⑤ Mix everything together for the dressing and stir through. Serve hot or cold as a salad.

Try adding other protein elements such as flaked fresh cooked salmon or chunks of cooked chicken.

Porcini and Truffle Bread

Ingredients

750g bread flour

7g fast action yeast

1 level teaspoon sugar

1 rounded teaspoon sea salt

2 tablespoons olive oil

Approximately 540ml warm water

Topping

50g dried porcini soaked in 50ml boiling water

1 fat garlic clove, finely grated with 1 teaspoon sea salt

1 tablespoon truffle (tartufo) paste

50g Parmesan, finely grated

1 teaspoon lemon zest

2 long stems rosemary, leaves finely chopped

¼ teaspoon black pepper

50ml olive oil

Serves 6-8

What you do

1 Place the flour in a large bowl, add the sugar and salt and with opened fingers, stir through with your hand to mix well. Add the yeast and repeat the mixing.

2 Now make a deep well in the centre and pour in the olive oil and about 350ml of the water. In a figure 8 movement fold the flour into the water and olive oil. DON'T OVER MIX!! You want a loose, soft dough, so don't force into a hard ball. Trickle in a little water at a time to achieve this soft, stretchy texture.

3 Wet your other hand and slide the dough from your mixing hand. Tip the dough onto an oiled surface. Wash your hands and then oil them. Pick up the dough and throw it onto the surface as if bowling a ball over-arm, but keeping hold of one end so the dough elongates when it hits the surface. Repeat this action about 20 times until the dough tightens and becomes smooth. Place on an oiled

tray and turn over so it is oiled on both sides. Lay a sheet of clingfilm over the top and leave it somewhere warm until doubled in size.

4 Bring the dough back to an oiled surface, pull the edges out and then fold them into the centre to create a large mushroom shape. Press down with your palms to expel some of the air bubbles. Place on an oiled tray and, working from the centre outwards, knuckle the dough to fill the tin, use your palms too. If the dough doesn't quite fit, leave it for 15 minutes and it will be easier.

5 Meanwhile, make the topping. Simply finely chop everything and mix together, and stir in the olive oil. When the dough is nice and springy use your fingers to make dimples, then smother the surface with the porcini mixture.

6 Bake in a preheated oven at 220°C/200°C Fan/Gas 7 for 20-25 minutes until risen and deliciously golden. Cool for 10 minutes on a rack before demolishing!

Also try: zesty gremolata topping

Mix together: 1 tablespoon chopped parsley, 1 tablespoon chopped coriander, 1 teaspoon each of orange and lemon zest, 2 fat garlic cloves finely grated with 1 teaspoon sea salt, 1 medium red chilli finely chopped and 4 tablespoons olive oil.

This is so delicious! Obviously you have to love fungi, but if you don't, try the gremolata version, it's really zesty and goes with most dishes.

Arancini with Blue Cheese and Winter Tomato Velouté

These are delicious stuffed risotto balls, coated in breadcrumbs and then deep-fried. They are a great treat to make and share with friends. The sauce makes this into a more sophisticated dish and the addition of a little seasonal salad balances everything nicely. Try the winter salad on page 90.

Ingredients

Risotto base

800ml good flavoured chicken or vegetable stock

250g Arborio rice

½ teaspoon sea salt

¼ teaspoon saffron

1 fat clove of garlic, finely grated

50g Parmesan cheese, grated

150g mozzarella, cut into small cubes

1 heaped tablespoon finely chopped herbs e.g. parsley and sage

Filling

1 tablespoon sundried tomato paste

75g gorgonzola or dolcelatte cheese, we love to use Perl Las

Coating

1 large free-range egg

170g plain flour

500g dried breadcrumbs, panko are great

Sunflower oil for frying

Serves 4

What you do

1 Bring the stock to the boil in a medium pan, then add the rice, salt and saffron. Bring back up to the boil, then turn down the heat and simmer on a medium heat until the stock has been absorbed. Stir in the grated parmesan, herbs and grated garlic and season to taste, then leave to cool completely, then pop it in the fridge.

2 Stir the mozzarella into the cool rice and check the seasoning. Wet your hands and take a tablespoonful of the mixture and roll it into a ball. Poke a hole in the middle and spoon in a little of the sun-dried tomato paste and a tiny cube of gorgonzola, then fill the hole with extra rice.

Repeat until all the rice is used up.

③ To coat the balls, beat together the egg, flour and enough water to make a thick batter (about 175ml), season this with ¼ teaspoon of sea salt and a pinch of pepper. Put the breadcrumbs onto a plate.

④ Fill a third of a large pan with oil, heat to 170°C, or until a breadcrumb sizzles gently in the oil. While the oil is heating up, dip each rice ball into the batter to coat, then onto the breadcrumbs, sprinkling them on top and pressing lightly to ensure they are well coated.

⑤ Cook in batches until golden brown, making sure the oil comes back up to temperature between batches. Drain on kitchen paper and sprinkle with a little sea salt while still warm.

⑥ These are delicious served with Winter Tomato Velouté (you will need just ½ the quantity) and a little salad. Try the winter salad on page 90, it goes really well with the arancini.

Winter Tomato Velouté

Ingredients

1 medium onion

2 fat garlic cloves

1 tablespoon olive oil

½ teaspoon sea salt

¼ teaspoon ground black pepper

3 sprigs of thyme

2 sprigs rosemary

500g tinned cherry tomatoes

1 tablespoon sun dried tomato paste

100ml white wine

100ml double cream

Sea salt and pepper to taste

Makes 650ml

What you do

1 Set your oven to 200°C/180°C Fan/Gas 6.

2 Line a small baking tin with parchment paper. Cut the onion into 8 wedges and slice the garlic cloves. Mix together with the olive oil, salt, pepper and pop the herbs underneath the onions so they don't burn. Roast in the oven for 20 minutes, stirring twice so they cook evenly.

3 When the onions have softened and slightly coloured, pour in the tomatoes and mix together, roast for a further 20-25 minutes until the mixture has thickened.

4 Remove and tip everything into a saucepan. Add the white wine and bring to the boil, stir in the cream and boil for 3 minutes.

This is great sauce for pasta, fish and chicken and you can add chopped fresh herbs, olives and chilli for a nice piquant finish.

5 Remove the sprigs of herbs, then using a stick blender whizz the tomatoes to form a smooth consistency.

6 Pass through a sieve into a small saucepan. Taste and season accordingly.

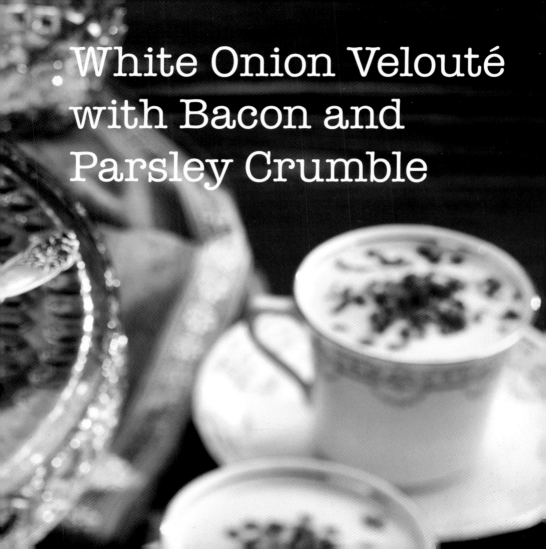

White Onion Velouté with Bacon and Parsley Crumble

Ingredients

100g salted butter

1kg large white onions, peeled and thinly sliced

350g potatoes, peeled and thinly sliced

300g leeks, white parts only, peeled and sliced thinly

2 fat garlic cloves, thinly sliced

2 sprigs thyme

1 bay leaf

750ml whole milk

1 litre good chicken or vegetable stock

200ml double cream

Bacon crumble

4 rashers good quality back bacon

1 tablespoon toasted breadcrumbs

1 tablespoon parsley

Pinch smoked sea salt (optional) – Halen Môn is wonderful

½ teaspoon white pepper

Serves 4-6 as a starter, half quantity will also make a lovely little soup shot at the beginning of a supper for 8 served in little cups or glass tumblers.

What you do

1 Melt the butter in a large saucepan, add the onions, stir through and cover directly with a piece of parchment paper or foil – a cartouche. Keep the heat low so they don't colour and cook until soft, stirring occasionally – about 20 minutes.

2 Once soft, add the potatoes, leeks, garlic, thyme, bay leaf and pepper and stir together. Pour in the milk and stock, bring to the boil then reduce the heat to a simmer and cook until the potatoes are soft. Stir in the cream.

3 Remove the sprigs of thyme and the bay leaf. Using a hand blender, blitz the ingredients to form a smooth, velvety soup.

4 To make the bacon crumble, place the slices of bacon on a baking sheet lined with foil, top with another sheet of foil and then another baking sheet to weight the bacon down. This will increase the temperature inside and the bacon will turn nice and crispy. Pop in the oven for 20-25 minutes at 200°C/180°C Fan/Gas 6. Remove from the baking sheet and drain on kitchen paper, it will crisp up as it cools. Chop the bacon and mix with the parsley and toasted breadcrumbs.

5 Serve the soup in warmed bowls and top with the bacon and parsley crumb.

Angela's note

Try this soup with a lovely mushroom and truffle caviar. Fry 100g finely chopped little portobello mushrooms in 15g butter until soft, stir in 1 dessertspoon of finely chopped reconstituted porcini, a sprinkle of sea salt and white pepper.

Finish with 1 teaspoon of truffle oil, a tablespoon of toasted breadcrumbs and one of chopped parsley.

Root Vegetable Pakora with Date and Tamarind Chutney

Ingredients

150g sweet potatoes, grated

100g beetroot (raw), grated

100g onion, very thinly sliced

100g kale or cabbage leaves, finely shredded

8 stems coriander, chopped

1 green finger chilli, finely chopped

1 tablespoon lemon juice

1 level teaspoon sea salt

150g gram flour

50g self-raising flour

½ teaspoon Kashmiri chilli

½ teaspoon garam masala

½ teaspoon tandoori masala

Sunflower oil for frying

Serves 4

What you do

1 Place all the prepared vegetables in a large bowl, add the chopped coriander, and chilli, the lemon juice and sea salt mix well. Taste to ensure the seasoning is ok, it should be well flavoured.

2 Sift in the gram and self-raising flour, add the chilli powder, garam masala and tandoori masala and stir well to combine. Carefully drizzle in just enough water to make a coating consistency on the vegetables. If it is too wet, add some more garam flour.

3 Use a teaspoon as a measure and scoop up 12 heaped portions of mixture into your hand. Roll each scoop into a ball, then flatten it slightly. Don't make them too big otherwise they will struggle to cook through properly.

4 Heat the oil in a deep, heavy-based frying pan, test the readiness of the heat with a piece of pakora, it should sizzle nice and gently, turn the heat down slightly if it browns too quickly.

5 Cook in batches until deep gold and crisp. Remove with a slotted spoon and drain well on kitchen paper. Serve with a yummy date and tamarind chutney.

Spiced Vegetable Pie

This is a hearty dish that brings together a tasty mix of seasonal vegetables, Arabic spices and a creamy luxurious topping.

Ingredients

1 small cauliflower

Sea salt

2 medium onions

2 tablespoons sunflower oil

300g butternut squash, grated

200g leeks, shredded

1 teaspoon fennel seeds, roasted and ground

2 teaspoons baharat spice mix (see recipe)

1 tablespoon tomato purée

Topping

200g natural Greek yoghurt

200g tahini paste

2 medium free-range eggs

1-2 tablespoons lemon juice

1-2 tablespoons water

2 tablespoons pine nuts or flaked almonds

1 tablespoon chopped parsley to finish

Serves 4

What you do

1 Break the cauliflower into florets and place in a saucepan of salted boiling water. Cook until just soft, drain well. Place in a shallow casserole or pan and flatten slightly with the back of a large spoon.

2 To prepare the rest of the vegetables, pour the oil into a frying pan and add the onions, sprinkle in ½ a teaspoon of sea salt and fry over a medium heat until they start to turn soft and golden. Add the butternut squash, leeks and another ½ teaspoon of sea salt, stir through, add a couple of tablespoons of water or vegetables stock to create steam. This will help the vegetables soften quickly.

3 When the butternut squash starts to brown, add the ground fennel and baharat spice mix, cook for 4 minutes, stirring occasionally. Stir in the tomato purée and simmer for another 3 minutes, the mixture will thicken and intensify in flavour. Spoon the mixture over the cauliflower and smooth over.

④ Make the topping by mixing together the yoghurt and tahini, beat in the eggs and lemon juice. Pour over the vegetables and sprinkle the top with pine nuts or flaked almonds. Bake in the oven for 20-25 minutes at 180°C/160°C Fan/Gas 4. The top should look golden and set. Finish with chopped parsley.

Baharat Spice mix

Ingredients

The word Baharat means "spice" in Arabic and used to flavour all manner of dishes from soups and pilafs, to marinades for meat, fish and vegetables. We use it a lot in our Middle Eastern courses and it's delicious.

2 tablespoons black peppercorns

1 teaspoon chilli flakes

2 tablespoons coriander seeds

2 tablespoons cumin seeds

1 tablespoon allspice berries

1 teaspoon cardamom seeds

2 whole cloves

4 (3-inch) cassia or cinnamon sticks

2 tablespoons ground sweet paprika

½ teaspoon freshly grated nutmeg

½ teaspoon turmeric

What you do

① Heat a large frying pan and add the whole spices, roast until fragrant, tip into a bowl and leave to cool.

② Grind to a powder using a spice grinder or mortar and pestle, stir in the paprika, nutmeg and turmeric. Store in an airtight container and keep for up to 3 months.

Smoked Sea Salt Caramel Pork Fillet, Egg Noodles, Greens and Soy

Ingredients

1 large pork tenderloin around 500g, trimmed and cut in half

Marinade

2 tablespoons fish sauce

1 tablespoon soy sauce

2 tablespoons lime juice

1 heaped teaspoon chopped ginger

3 fat garlic cloves, finely grated with ½ teaspoon sea salt

2 teaspoons palm sugar

1 dessertspoon rapeseed oil

Sauce

2 tablespoons dark muscavado sugar

½ teaspoon smoked sea salt (Halen Môn is perfect)

2 tablespoons lime juice

1 large red chilli, sliced

8 stems of fresh coriander, stems finely chopped, leaves left whole

Serves 4

What you do

1 To prepare the pork, mix together the fish sauce, soy, lime juice, ginger, garlic and sugar. Place in a poly bag and pour in the marinade, mix around so everything mingles then pop in the fridge for at least an hour. Overnight gives a deeper flavour to the pork.

2 To cook, take the meat from the fridge an hour before cooking so it comes to room temperature. Heat the rapeseed oil in a skillet pan and sear the meat to brown all over. Reduce the heat to low/medium and cook for 3 minutes on each side making quarter turns, so 12 minutes in all. Remove the pork and rest, covered loosely with foil.

3 Add the marinade to the pan and cook over a medium heat, it should bubble gently. Stir in the muscavado sugar and salt, wait for it to dissolve then add the lime juice, chilli and coriander stems. Add a couple of

tablespoons of water if the sauce becomes too thick.

④ To serve, slice the pork on the angle, pour over the sauce. Finish with the coriander leaves. Flat rice noodles and Asian style greens are perfect with this.

Asian Style Greens

Ingredients

1 dessertspoon sesame oil

400g greens: bok choy, long stem broccoli, cabbage leaves or spinach

1 teaspoon sesame oil

3 tablespoons vegetable or chicken stock

1 tablespoon lime juice

1 dessertspoon toasted sesame seeds

What you do

① Bring a pan of water to the boil, add ½ teaspoon sea salt.

② Trim and wash the greens, plunge into the water and cook for about 5-7 minutes until tender. Drain well.

③ Plate and finish with a mixture of the sesame oil, stock and lime juice. Sprinkle with the toasted sesame seeds.

We love serving this around Chinese New Year. It is perfectly balanced and packed full of flavours that invigorate the palette.

Barbecued Hot Smoked Salmon with Rosti and Coriander Relish

This is a great recipe to wow your friends next time you have a BBQ. We have a Weber Grill Academy at the Cookery School and we barbecue all year round. This is my first recipe inspired by their method of cooking - but it works just as well in a conventional oven.

Ingredients

4 salmon fillets, skin removed

Rub

1 teaspoon sweet paprika

1 dessertspoon Dijon mustard

1 tablespoon lemon juice

1 teaspoon maple syrup

Rosti

300g sweet potato, peeled and grated

300g celeriac, peeled and grated

1 tablespoon grated onion

1 heaped teaspoon curry powder

2 large egg yolks

1 teaspoon sea salt

¼ teaspoon black pepper

Rapeseed oil for brushing

Coriander Relish

1 small bunch coriander

2 medium green chillies

2 fat cloves garlic, peeled and grated

2 tablespoons Greek style yoghurt

2-3 tablespoons lime juice

¼ teaspoon sea salt

Smoking

2 handfuls of cherry wood chips

Serves 4

What you do

1 First, make the coriander relish. Finely chop the coriander stems and roughly chop the leaves, place in a mixing bowl. Add all the other ingredients and mix well. Cover and pop in the fridge so that the flavours mingle nicely for at least an hour.

2 Next, make the rub for the salmon. Simply mix everything together and smear over the fillets and place on a BBQ tray lined with parchment paper. Keep in the fridge until needed. We use Weber Grill Trays, which are perfect for even cooking and smoking.

3 Cooking on your BBQ – half fill your BBQ chimney with charcoals, light and leave for 15-20 minutes, then tip into charcoal baskets and separate them, placing at either side of the interior to create an indirect cooking method. Place a cast iron pan on the grill to heat up for cooking the rosti, pop the BBQ lid on and leave it to come to temperature, around 180°C-200°C. Soak the cherry wood chips in water ready for smoking.

4 Meanwhile, prepare the rosti. Get a large mixing bowl, add the grated sweet potato, celeriac and onion. Stir in the curry powder, egg yolks, sea salt and black pepper. To cook the rosti, lightly brush the hot grill pan with rapeseed oil and place 4 heaped tablespoons of the mixture on to the pan and flatten out with the back of the spoon. Replace the lid and cook for about 6 minutes, check the underside is golden brown before flipping them over, replace the lid and cook for another 6 minutes. The rosti should be cooked through and golden. Keep warm in the oven whilst you cook the salmon. Alternatively, these can be cooked in a griddle pan on your hob.

5 Now for the salmon. Place the grill tray on the BBQ and add a handful of soaked cherry wood chips directly on to the coals. Close the BBQ lid and cook for 15 minutes, then check the internal temperature of the salmon – it should be around 60°C. Remove and rest for 5 minutes, the salmon will be just cooked through and deliciously succulent.

6 Alternatively roast in a preheated oven at 200°C/180°C Fan/Gas 6 for 15-20 minutes. Use smoked paprika in place of sweet in the rub to give a smoky flavour.

Fritto Misto with Salsa Verde and Aioli

There is a plethora of seafood available in the winter months and this recipe is such a great way to take advantage of that. The delicious, crisp, light batter and the dipping sauces make it the perfect sociable food to share with fiends and family.

Ingredients

2 prepared squid, portioned into rings, tentacles separated

16 medium raw tiger prawn tails, peeled, deveined, tail fans intact

400g white fish fillets e.g. hake, bass, sole or plaice, cut into 2cm pieces

8 thin slices of sweet potato, cut with a vegetable peeler

8 finger-length strips of leek

8 sage leaves

Batter

150g self-raising flour

1 tablespoon cornflour

½ teaspoon bicarbonate of soda

½ teaspoon cayenne pepper

½ teaspoon lemon zest

1 level teaspoon sea salt, you may like a little more to taste

½ teaspoon white pepper

350-375ml chilled water

Sunflower oil, for deep-frying

Lemon wedges, to serve

Serves 4

What you do

1 Spread the seafood out on a large plate and pat dry with kitchen paper.

2 Make the batter by sifting together the self-raising flour, cornflour, bicarbonate of soda and cayenne pepper into a bowl, stir in the lemon zest, sea salt and pepper, slowly whisk in 350ml chilled water to form a smooth batter.

3 Half fill a deep-fryer or large saucepan with oil and heat to 190°C. Oil is hot enough when it turns a cube of bread golden in around 30 seconds.

4 Cook everything in batches, start with the vegetables. Dip into batter and quickly slide up the side of the bowl to allow excess batter to run off, ease into the oil and fry until golden, carefully moving them around to ensure that the pieces

don't clump together.

(5) Remove and drain on kitchen paper and keep warm in the oven until everything is cooked. Sprinkle with sea salt and serve with lemon wedges.

Aioli
Ingredients

3 tablespoons good mayonnaise

1 tablespoon lemon juice

1 tablespoon Greek style yoghurt

3 fat garlic cloves, grated

½ teaspoon sea salt (we love Halen Môn roasted garlic sea salt for extra oomph!)

¼ teaspoon freshly ground black pepper

What you do

You can make this in advance and keep in the fridge until the cooking starts. Simply mix everything together, taste and adjust the seasoning to suit your palette.

Salsa Verde
Ingredients

8 stems flat-leaf parsley, stems and leaves chopped

3 stems mint, leaves chopped

2 tablespoons capers, drained and chopped

3 anchovy fillets in oil, drained and chopped

1 fat garlic clove, grated

1 heaped teaspoon Dijon mustard

1-2 tablespoons lemon juice

120-150ml extra virgin olive oil

What you do

You can make the salsa verde some time in advance. Mix everything together, taste and adjust with lemon juice and a little sea salt if needed.

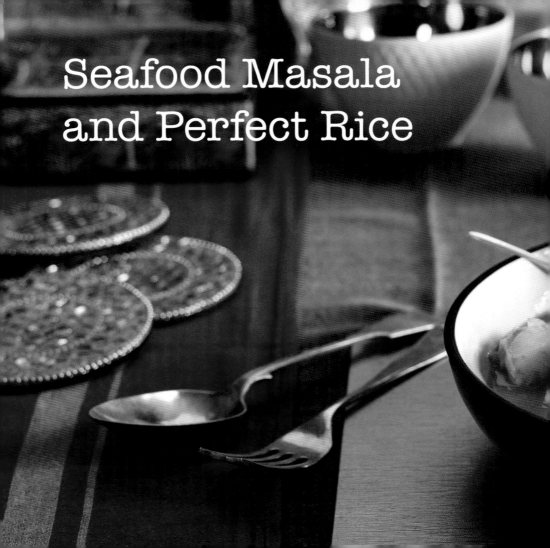

Seafood Masala and Perfect Rice

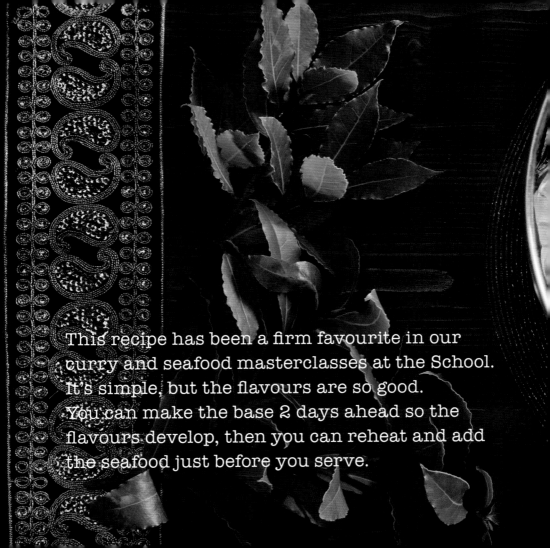

This recipe has been a firm favourite in our curry and seafood masterclasses at the School. It's simple, but the flavours are so good. You can make the base 2 days ahead so the flavours develop, then you can reheat and add the seafood just before you serve.

Ingredients

Spice mix

1 tablespoon coriander seeds

1 tablespoon cumin seeds

1 tablespoons fennel seeds

½ teaspoon black peppercorns

1 teaspoon turmeric

1 rounded teaspoon Kashmiri chilli powder

1 flat teaspoon sweet paprika

Curry

2 tablespoons coconut oil

1 large onion, finely chopped

1 tablespoon chopped ginger

4 fat garlic cloves, finely grated with 1 teaspoon sea salt

4 sprigs fresh curry leaves

1 teaspoon black mustard seeds

1 piece cassia bark

120g chopped tinned tomatoes

1 tablespoon tamarind paste

1 dessertspoon palm sugar or jaggery

300ml good fish stock (see step 2)

500ml thick coconut milk

8 stems fresh coriander, chopped

1 tablespoon lime juice to finish

Seafood

600g of fish fillets cut into good sized chunks. Try hake, monk or haddock

12 large whole raw black tiger prawns, peeled, shells and head reserved

1 medium squid, cleaned and cut into rings, use tentacles too!

A couple of handfuls of live mussels, cleaned and de-bearded

1 tablespoon chopped coriander

Serves 4

....

What you do

1 First, make the spice mix. Dry roast the whole spices in a warm pan until fragrant. Tip into a bowl and cool. Spoon into a spice grinder and whizz to a powder. Mix in the turmeric and paprika to finish.

2 Make a simple fish stock by placing the prawn heads and shells in a saucepan with any fish skin. Add a small chopped onion, carrot and a celery stick and a teaspoon of sea salt, a slice of lemon, some parsley stalks, 60ml white wine and 500ml water. Boil for 20 minutes, strain into a pan and bring back to the boil and reduce to 300ml. Cook the mussels in the stock until they open, only cook ones that are closed and discard any that don't open after cooking. Remove with a slotted spoon, the lovely juice from the mussels will be in the stock and you can remove the mussel meat from the shells easily, ready to add to the curry.

3 To make the curry, heat the coconut oil in a large pan, add the onion and cook slowly over a medium heat until really soft and slightly golden and sticky. Stir in the ginger, garlic, curry leaves, mustard seeds and cassia bark, cook for about a minute. Now add

the ground spice mix – this will dry in the pan quickly so keep stirring and cook for a minute, add a couple of tablespoons of the stock to create a paste and continue cooking for 3 minutes. Stir in the tomatoes, tamarind and palm sugar and simmer for a couple of minutes. Then pour in the stock and coconut milk, bring to the boil and then reduce the heat so it simmers. Cook until the liquid has reduced and thickened slightly.

4 Add the seafood, starting with the chunks of fish, push under the sauce – from here on, don't stir; otherwise the fish will break up. Cook for 3 minutes then add the prawns, pushing them under the sauce. When they turn pink, add the squid and finally the cooked mussels. The curry should be gently simmering throughout the cooking of the seafood.

5 Taste and season with salt and lime juice. Sprinkle with fresh coriander and serve with perfect rice.

Perfect Rice

Measure out all the ingredients correctly and follow all the steps to perfection!

Ingredients

25g salted butter

3 pieces cassia bark

1 black cardamom pod

1 teaspoon cumin seeds

½ teaspoon chilli flakes

340g basmati rice

450ml boiling water or vegetable stock

Serves 4

....

What you do

1 Rinse the rice in a sieve until the water runs clear, tip into a bowl, cover with cold water and soak for half an hour.

2 To cook the rice, first drain in a sieve. Melt the butter in a large pan over a medium heat, add the spices and cook for 2 minutes. Add the rice followed by boiling water or stock. Bring the pan to the boil then place a tight fitting lid on top or use a sheet of foil, then a lid.

3 Boil for a couple of seconds, then reduce the heat to the minimum and cook for 20-25 minutes – put your timer on. And don't peek before the time is up!

4 When the time is up, the rice will have soaked up all the spice-infused liquid. Rake it gently with a fork to separate the grains and serve.

The secret to cooking great rice is to follow the steps, make sure the temperature is low before you cover it for the cooking time, and don't peek until 20 minutes is up. Off the heat, it will still be cooking, so don't be tempted to leave it too long!

Toad in the Hole with Apple and Sage

This is a great British classic and real winter comfort food. Choose really good butcher's pork sausages and bacon to get the full meaty flavour. The addition of onions, apples, prunes and sage take this Toad to a whole new level!

Ingredients

Batter

4 free-range eggs

300g plain flour

300ml whole milk

300ml cold water

1 rounded tablespoon wholegrain mustard

The Toad

8 best quality butcher's pork sausages

8 thin slices good quality streaky bacon

1 large red onion, sliced

1 yummy eating apple, quartered and sliced

8 soft ready-to-eat prunes or apricots

12 sage leaves

3 tablespoons dripping – ask your butcher!

Serves 4

What you do

1 First, make the batter. Sift the flour into a mixing bowl, make a well in the centre and crack in the eggs, pour in the milk and water and beat together. Gradually whisk in the flour to give a smooth batter that resembles single cream. Stir in the mustard, cover and leave to rest for 15 minutes.

2 Preheat the oven to 200°C/180°C Fan/Gas 6.

3 Put the dripping in a roasting tin and pop in the oven until it is really hot, almost smoking!

4 First, add the sausages and roast for 7 minutes, then add the bacon, onion and apple slices. Roast for another 7 minutes.

5 Increase the oven temperature to 220°C/200°C Fan/Gas 7. Remove the roasting tin from the oven, add the prunes, whisk up the batter and pour in. Return to the oven and

bake for about 25-30 minutes until puffed and golden. Serve with white onion sauce and a simple seasonal vegetable.

....

White Onion Sauce

Ingredients

3 large onions, peeled and thinly sliced

50g salted butter

30g plain flour

300ml whole milk

½ teaspoon fresh grated nutmeg

75ml double cream

Sea salt and white pepper

What you do

1 Melt the butter in a large sauté pan, add the onions, stir through the butter and gently fry them over a low heat until really soft, but not brown.

2 Next, sprinkle the flour over the onions and stir through, cook for 1 minute. Remove from the heat and slowly add the milk, mixing well to avoid lumps.

3 Place back on to the heat and, whilst stirring constantly, bring to the boil then reduce the heat. The sauce should be really creamy in consistency. To finish, add the nutmeg, then sea salt and white pepper to taste. Finally, stir in the cream, reheat gently and then serve.

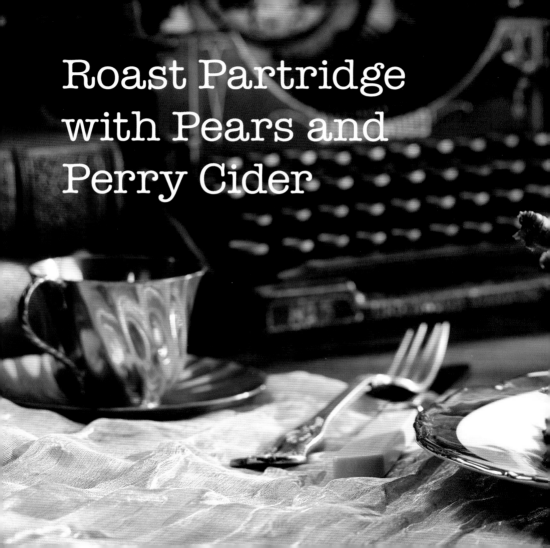

Roast Partridge with Pears and Perry Cider

Ingredients

4 young, plump partridge

6 sprigs of thyme

12 juniper berries

1 level teaspoon sea salt

8 peppercorns

100g Welsh salted butter

8 thin rashers of good quality streaky bacon

2 small firm, but ripe, pears

2 tablespoons lemon juice

4 small thick slices of rustic white bread + some butter

2 tablespoons redcurrant, blackberry, rowan or quince jelly

120ml perry cider – I love Gwynt-Y-Ddraig Perry Vale

Serves 4

What you do

1 Check the partridge are in good shape – no stray feathers, broken bones or shot pellets. Set the oven at 220°C/180°C Fan/Gas 7.

2 Use a pestle and mortar or a sharp knife and a board to prepare a little aromatic rub. Pull the leaves from the thyme stems and mash pound or chop together with the juniper berries, sea salt and peppercorns. Mix with ¾ of the butter. Spread all over the birds, heavily on the breasts.

3 Lay the bacon slices on your prep board then stretch them with the flat of a knife blade to make them longer and thinner. Wrap them around the birds forming an "X" shape. Place in a roasting tin.

4 To prepare the pears, cut each one into 6 wedges, and drizzle with the lemon juice. Melt the remaining butter in a non-stick pan, add the pears and sauté until lightly golden,

then add to the pan with the birds. Roast for 20 minutes, then remove the bacon (chop it up and keep to use at the end), pop the birds back in the oven for another 10 minutes. Alternatively, you can leave the bacon on as a garnish.

5 To make little bread croutons, spread the slices of bread with butter and bake in the oven for 15 minutes until crisp and golden.

To serve

6 Remove the birds, place on the croutons and keep warm, keep the bacon and pears warm while you make the sauce.

7 Put the roasting tin with the juices over a medium heat, stir in the jelly of your choice and let it melt and bubble, pour in the perry and stir to dissolve any sticky residue, this will add to the flavour.

8 Plate the croutons and birds, add the pears at the side, sprinkle with chopped bacon, or leave the bacon on the birds and spoon over the delicious sauce.

I love game, it's so flavourful and versatile. We use it at the School in many ways, from tandoori on the BBQ to a classic raised pie. This recipe is a lovely supper dish for friends.

Game Tagine

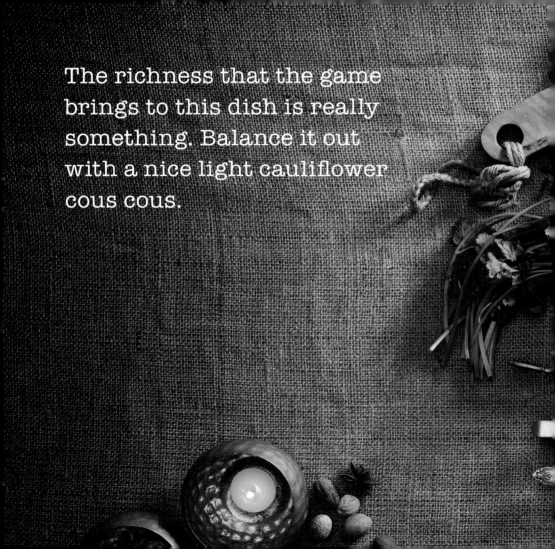

The richness that the game brings to this dish is really something. Balance it out with a nice light cauliflower cous cous.

Ingredients

1.5-2kg mixed game cuts e.g. pheasant, mallard, venison, wild boar etc.

Spice paste

2 tablespoons ras el hanout

½ teaspoon chilli powder, more if you like it hot

4 fat garlic cloves, finely grated with a little sea salt

2 tablespoons argan or rapeseed oil

The rest

150g salted butter, cut into small pieces

1 large onion, cut into 8 wedges

2 large carrots, peeled and cut into thick rounds

1 small butternut squash, peeled and cut into cubes or wedges

100g soft, dried, apricots, cut in half

1 tablespoon agarve syrup or maple syrup

150ml white wine

1 tablespoon cider vinegar

1 small bunch fresh coriander, chopped stems, keep the leaves for serving

Serves 4

What you do

1 Pre-heat the oven to 150°C/130°C Fan fan/Gas 3.

2 Mix the ras el hanout spice with the chilli, garlic and 2 tablespoons of oil to form a paste.

3 Cut the game into similar sized chunks, make a small slit into each piece with a sharp knife – this will allow more spice flavour to get into the meat. Place the game in a large bowl with the vegetables and add the spice paste, mix everything really well to coat all the ingredients.

4 Heat a large pan and add ½ the butter, melt it over a medium heat.

When it starts to foam, add the meat and vegetables in batches and cook until lightly brown. Remove with a slotted spoon into a large tagine or casserole dish. Add the wine to the pan and dissolve away any juices, then pour this over the game. Add the apricots, maple syrup, vinegar, and remaining butter with 60ml of water and the chopped coriander stems. Cover with a lid and cook for 4 hours.

5 To finish the dish, roughly chop the coriander leaves and sprinkle over the top.

Serving Suggestion

I like to serve this dish with cauliflower cous cous, it balances the richness of this dish perfectly. Simply blitz the white florets of a medium cauliflower in food processor until it resembles cous cous. Steam for 10 minutes until tender, season and serve.

Sticky Duck with Shredded Leek Pancakes

This is another recipe that works really well on the BBQ, but also in the oven. The preparation may seem a little involved, but fun! Why not try it as a fun twist on Shrove Tuesday?

Ingredients

Approximately 2kg whole duck
2 tablespoons sea salt
1 tablespoon black pepper
1 teaspoon five-spice powder
2 teaspoons garlic granules
2 tablespoons molasses
2 tablespoons pomegranate molasses

Pancakes

125g plain flour
2 level teaspoons baking powder
1 teaspoon sea salt
2 medium free-range eggs, beaten
375ml whole milk
40g Welsh salted butter
1 medium leek, shredded finely
Hoisin sauce to serve

Serves 4-6

What you do

1 Preheat your oven to 240°C/220°C Fan/Gas 9, or prepare a full chimney of charcoal and light – when the coals are ready tip into BBQ baskets and set for indirect cooking.

2 First, make the pancakes. Sift the flour, baking powder and salt into a bowl, make a well in the centre and add the eggs. Start whisking and gradually pour in the milk and melted butter to form a smooth batter. Cover and leave to rest for an hour.

3 To prepare the duck, pat the duck all over with kitchen paper to dry. Next, get your hair dryer and blow-dry the duck for 5 minutes all over.

4 Mix together the sea salt, black pepper, five-spice powder and garlic granules, rub half of it over the duck, then blow-dry again for 5 minutes. Rub with the remaining dry mix ready for cooking.

5 To cook the duck, place the duck on a rack that fits inside a roasting tin and roast for 20 minutes

then reduce the temperature to 180°C/160°C Fan/Gas 4 and cook for a further 15 minutes per 450g.

6 If barbecuing, cook at 200°C for 20 minutes per 450g, check the internal temperature with a probe – it should be at 70°C.

7 For the glaze, when you reach the last 20 minutes of cooking mix together the molasses and pomegranate molasses and quickly brush all over the duck, return to the oven/BBQ and this will form a lovely glaze. When the duck is cooked remove and loosely cover with foil and leave to rest.

8 Meanwhile, cook the pancakes. Heat an oiled non-stick pan, add about 3 tablespoons of batter to cover the base of the pan thinly. Sprinkle a little of the shredded leek in, cook for about 2 minutes until golden brown underneath, then turn over and cook for 30 seconds. Remove and tip onto a warm plate, continue until all the batter is used up.

9 To serve, shred the duck and garnish with cucumber and mango salsa (see below), serve with the pancakes and hoisin sauce.

Cucumber and Mango Salsa

Ingredients

1 medium cucumber

1 large mango

1 medium red chilli

1 fat garlic clove, grated

12 stems coriander, chopped

3-4 tablespoons lime juice

What you do

Cut the cucumber in half and use a wide vegetable peeler to create long strips. Thinly slice the mango, place in a bowl with the cucumber and the rest of the ingredients, mix well.

Welsh Beef Osso Bucco with Gremolata

Slow cooked deliciousness,
perfect for a cold winter's day.
I am really particular when
it comes to sourcing meat.
Our butcher supplies us with
PGI (Protected Geographical
Indication) Welsh Lamb and Beef
and we use beef shin cut for this
dish in place of veal and it is
simply stunning in flavour,
every time.

Ingredients

4 thick slices osso bucco, use Welsh beef or rose veal shin

1 tablespoon plain flour

1 level teaspoon sea salt

½ teaspoon black pepper

30g butter

2 tablespoons olive oil

1 small onion, peeled and chopped very finely

1 small stick celery, chopped finely

150ml dry white wine

300ml light chicken or veal stock

For the gremolata

1 small unwaxed lemon, zest only, grated

1 fat garlic clove, peeled and finely chopped

4 stems parsley, chopped

Serves 4

What you do

1 Place the osso bucco on your prep board and pat both sides dry with kitchen paper. Mix the flour, salt and pepper together and lightly dust the meat all over.

2 Use a large frying pan for sealing the meat – heat the oil and lightly brown the osso bucco on both sides. Remove the meat and set aside.

3 Add the butter to the pan and then add the onion and celery, stir through and sauté over a low-medium heat. Add a couple of tablespoons of water or stock to steam fry. When the vegetables are soft, add the wine and cook off the alcohol, this takes about 30 seconds.

4 Add the osso bucco back into the pan, pour in the stock and bring to the boil. Reduce the heat to a very gentle simmer. Cook for about 1½ hours until the meat is really tender and almost falling off the bone.

Carefully turn the osso bucco over at 20-minute intervals so it cooks evenly and stays in one piece with the marrow intact.

5 Whilst the osso bucco is cooking, make the gremolata by mixing everything together, set aside until needed.

6 Serve the osso bucco on warm plates, spoon over the lovely sauce and sprinkle with the gremolata. I love this dish with soft polenta and greens, but a lovely creamy mash would do very nicely too.

BBQ Turkey Crown with a Smoked Chilli Glaze

The results you can achieve on a BBQ are astonishing. The turkey in this recipe is moist and succulent with a delicious crisp smoky skin. Great for a gathering.

Ingredients

5½kg de-boned turkey crown

Brine

2 litres Welsh cider, I love Gwynt-Y-Ddraig Farmhouse Cloudy Scrumpy

2 litres apple juice

1 large onion, sliced

2 bay leaves

1 teaspoon allspice

1 tablespoon coriander seeds

4 cloves

1 heaped teaspoon chilli flakes

200g sea salt

Glaze

240ml cider vinegar

½ teaspoon ground cloves

½ teaspoon ground star anise

½ teaspoon ground allspice

1 tablespoon ground coriander

1 medium onion, finely diced

1 rounded tablespoon of roasted garlic pulp (roast a bulb in the oven)

2 tablespoons rapeseed oil

120g dark muscovado sugar

2 tablespoons molasses

120g chipotle chilli paste

6 tablespoons tomato purée

1 tablespoon Worcestershire sauce

1-2 level teaspoons sea salt

Smoking

2 big handfuls of woodchips

Serves 6-8

What you do

This is a 2-day job in preparation, but it's worth it for a special gathering.

First, brine the turkey crown

Mix all the ingredients for the brine together in a large bowl or container. Add the turkey, cover and brine in the fridge for 24 hours. Before you cook the turkey, remove from the brine at least 8 hours before cooking. This allows the surface of the bird to dry and the end result will give a crisp bronze skin. Drain the turkey well, pat dry, then leave on the lowest shelf in the fridge, uncovered. I do this overnight (8 hours).

The glaze

Pour the vinegar into a saucepan and add the ground spices, simmer gently and reduce the liquid by half. Heat the oil in a skillet pan and sauté the onion until soft and lightly golden, then stir in the garlic and cook for a further 2 minutes. Add the sugar and molasses and stir through. When it starts to bubble gently, carefully tip it into the pan with the spiced vinegar. Add the chipotle paste, tomato purée and Worcestershire sauce and cook really gently for an hour, if it becomes too thick at any point, thin it with water. The consistency should be like a creamy paste so when you paint it on the turkey it doesn't run off.

To cook the turkey

1 Remove from the fridge and allow it to come to room temperature – about an hour. Soak 2 good handfuls of wood chips ready for smoking.

2 Set your BBQ up and light a full chimney of charcoal. When the coals are ready, tip them into charcoal baskets and place one at either side of the BBQ kettle, or tip into 2 heaps, one at each side to create an indirect heat, place the lid on the BBQ and allow the temperature to come to 200°C.

3 Roll up the turkey crown and secure with trussing string evenly spaced along the meat. Pat all over with kitchen paper once again to ensure it is dry – now you're ready to BBQ.

4 Place the turkey crown in the middle of the grill and quickly add the wood chips directly onto the charcoal, pop the lid on and let the smoking commence. Roast for 3 hours.

5 Baste the turkey with the smoked chilli sauce at 15 minute intervals during the last hour. This will allow a lovely sticky glaze to build up on the skin. Check the internal temperature before removing from the BBQ. it should be at 75°C-80°C. Rest for 20-30 minutes before carving (the temperature at the core will go up slightly during resting time).

6 I like to put a drip tray underneath with 200ml of water to collect all the juices and then make a simple sauce from it.

Chicken
Pastilla and
Winter Salad

This dish takes a little time, but it's so worth it. The result is crisp buttery pastry and succulent chicken with a rich hit of fruit and spice.

Ingredients

Serves 4

1kg free-range chicken thighs on the bone

1 teaspoon sea salt

1 level teaspoon cracked black pepper

150g medjool dates, pitted and halved

50g soft dried apricots, halved

50g dried sour cherries

3 large onions, peeled and sliced

2 cinnamon sticks

2 dried red chilles

2 tablespoons ras el hanout

240ml water

2 tablespoons chopped herbs e.g. parsley, coriander, mint

1 pack filo pastry

60g salted butter, melted

What you do

1 Place a large pan on a medium heat, when hot put the chicken thighs in skin side down, sprinkle with the ½ teaspoon sea salt and pepper, cook for about 15 minutes until golden then turn them over and cook for 5 minutes. Remove (reserving any chicken fat rendered from the cooking) and place in a roasting tin with the dates, apricots and cherries.

2 Add the onions to the frying pan and stir through the chicken fat, add another flat teaspoon of sea salt. Add a little water to help the onions cook evenly. When they are super soft and lightly golden, add

the cinnamon sticks, chilli and ras el hanout and mix through. Cook for about 30 seconds then add the water and bring to the boil, pour over the chicken thighs, cover with foil tightly and bake in the centre of the oven at 200°C/180°C Fan/Gas 6 for 1 hour.

3 Remove the foil carefully – hot steam will escape. The chicken should be falling off the bone – continue cooking for a further 10-15 minutes if it needs it.

4 Remove from the oven and carefully tip the contents into a large sieve over a bowl to separate the juice. Pull the chicken from the bones, discard the skin, bones and cartilage. Remove the cinnamon sticks and mix the chicken together with the dates, onions and fresh herbs, plus enough liquid to bind it into a paste like consistency. Keep the remaining juice.

5 To assemble the pastilla, butter 4 sheets of filo and place on a baking sheet overlapping to form one big sheet. Butter another sheet and fold in quarters, place this in the centre to form the base and then repeat the first step with another 4 overlapping sheets. Pile the chicken mixture into the middle of the filo and flatten slightly on top. Pull up the edges to meet in the centre sealing everything inside like a parcel. Brush with butter and bake in the oven at 200°C/180°C Fan/Gas 6 until deep golden and crisp.

6 Serve with a winter salad and the reserved juice.

Winter Salad

Ingredients

1 small savoy cabbage (or any other nice cabbage) quartered and central core removed

¼ small red onion thinly sliced and soaked in water for 20 minutes

2 sticks celery

A handful of spinach, shredded

1 delicious eating apple

A good handful of nuts – pistachio, walnut, hazelnut, almond

A few apricots, chopped (optional)

A tablespoon dried blueberries, cranberries or cherries (optional)

1 orange (blood oranges are delicious), segmented

1 small bunch of fresh herbs, coriander is delicious in this

½ teaspoon sea salt

¼ teaspoon black pepper

Dressing

2 tablespoons pomegranate molasses

2 tablespoons date molasses or runny honey/maple syrup

100ml apple/orange juice

Serves 4-6

What you do

1 Wash the cabbage leaves, remove the ribs from the larger outer leaves. Place one on top of the other and roll up into a fat cigar shape. Now cut thin slices, this will result in fine shreds, pop into a large mixing bowl. Drain the soaked onions – soaking mellows the flavour so it doesn't dominate.

2 Trim the celery, remove the fibrous strings along the back with

a peeler, slice finely and add to the cabbage and onion.

③ Quarter the apple and remove the core, slice thinly and add to the salad.

④ Chop the nuts and then dry roast in a pan until aromatic and slightly browned. Add to the salad.

⑤ Add apricots, dried berries, orange segments, chopped coriander, salt and pepper.

⑥ Cover and store in the fridge until needed. Mix the dressing ingredients together. To serve, simply add the dressing to the salad and toss through. Goes with everything, but delicious on its own too!

Also try adding shredded celeriac, beetroot and carrot for vivid colour and different flavours.

Holee Molee

This is a chilli I remember making when the lovely Jay Rayner came to the School to present a cooking challenge for *The One Show* (we did a lot of these over 2 years and it was good fun). He ate 3 large bowls! I think he liked it.

Ingredients

2 tablespoons rapeseed oil

700g trimmed Welsh shin beef, cut into large cubes

2 medium onions, finely diced

2 medium carrots, peeled sliced and finely diced

2 sticks celery, finely diced

2 small red or yellow peppers, deseeded and chopped

2 fat garlic cloves, grated

2 small fresh green chillies, finely chopped

3 chipotle chillies

2 ancho chillies

1½ teaspoons freshly ground cumin

1½ teaspoons smoked paprika

1½ teaspoons dried oregano

1½ teaspoons raw cacao powder

300ml freshly brewed coffee

750ml good beef stock – canned beef consommé is great

400g tinned tomatoes, chopped

Serves 4

What you do

1 Heat the oil in a heavy-based pan, add the chunks of beef in batches and brown on all sides over a medium-high heat, don't burn, just brown.

2 Remove with a slotted spoon onto a plate. Add the onions to the pan and fry until they are soft and golden brown (add a few tablespoons of water or stock to steam fry, this will quicken the cooking process), then add the chopped carrot, celery, and pepper, stir together then cover with a lid and cook over a medium heat until soft.

3 Next, stir in the garlic and fresh green chilli, cook for a couple of minutes.

4 Remove the stalks and seeds from the chipotle chillies and ancho

chillies (if using dried chillies, soak in boiled water for 20 minutes to soften), finely chop them and add to the pot. Then add the rest of the ingredients in order, stirring well and leave to simmer with the lid on for 2 hours, occasionally stirring.

5 After two hours take the lid off the pot and let the sauce reduce down for about 30 minutes. The beef should now be very tender. If the sauce is a little thin, thicken with some tomato purée. Check the seasoning.

6 I serve this in bowls with fresh avocado salsa, and homemade tortilla chips – delish!

For a vegetarian version, substitute the weight of meat with a combination of cubed squash and chopped mushrooms. Use a heaped teaspoon of chopped porcini to add good flavour to the dish, plus Marigold Swiss Vegetable Powder to make your stock.

Panzerotti

The pasta can be
cut into tagliatelle,
pappardelle or sheets
and used in a classic
lasagna or cannelloni.

Ingredients

Pasta

340g 00 flour

160g semolina flour

Large pinch of fine sea salt

3 large eggs and 2 or 3 egg yolks, at room temperature, lightly beaten (if the mixture doesn't come together with 2 yolks, add the third)

Filling

150g butternut squash or pumpkin

75g onion

1 fat garlic clove

1 heaped teaspoon lemon zest – a little juice to season

50g ricotta, drained

25g taleggio or dolcelatte cheese

25g Parmesan

¼ teaspoon fresh grated nutmeg

1 dessertspoon toasted pine nuts or chopped toasted almonds

2 amaretti biscuits, crushed

Sea salt and white pepper to season

To finish

1 tablespoon olive oil

50g salted butter

12 sage leaves, chopped

1 teaspoon lemon zest

Grated Parmesan

Serves 4

What you do

1 Mix the flours together and tip out onto your surface in a mound, sprinkle with the salt. Make a large well in the middle and pour in two thirds of the eggs.

2 Using your fingertips in a circular motion, gradually stir in the flour until you have a soft dough. Add more egg if needed. Knead for about 10 minutes until it is smooth, and springs back when poked. Divide the dough in two and wrap in a damp cloth. Leave to rest for about an hour in a cool place.

3 Meanwhile, make the filling. Line a roasting tin or dish with

parchment paper. Cut the squash or pumpkin into small, even-sized cubes, chop the onion and slice the garlic. Place the ingredients into the tin and drizzle with a little olive oil, mix through to coat the ingredients then roast for about 25-30 minutes until lightly golden and soft. Remove and tip everything into a bowl, mash it all together and leave to cool.

4 Mix in the lemon zest and a dessertspoon of lemon juice (you may wish to add a little more when you taste once the filling is finished). Mix in the ricotta and taleggio or dolcelatte, Parmesan, pine nuts and amaretti biscuits and season to your taste. The filling should be really flavourful so it shines through the pasta.

5 To make the panzerotti, roll out the first ball of dough on a lightly floured surface until it is about 1cm thick, so it will go through the widest setting of your pasta machine. Put it through each setting twice, until you can see your fingers through the pasta sheet. Cut it in half when it becomes too long to handle. Store the other half under a damp cloth while you work on the first batch.

6 Cut the rolled-out pasta into rounds using a small serrated edged cutter, do this closely together so you get as many as you can from the sheet. Dampen the edges of each pasta round, spoon ½ a teaspoon of the filling onto one half of each round, fold over and seal to form a little pasty shape. Place on a floured board or tray whilst you work on the rest, this will prevent them sticking.

7 To cook the panzerotti, bring a large pan of salted water to the boil. Add the panzerotti, they will sink at first, then float to the top and lighten in colour as cooking progresses. They should take about 4-5 minutes, drain really well.

8 To finish the dish, heat the olive oil and butter in the pasta pan, add the chopped sage and lemon zest, cook gently for 2 minutes. Tip in the panzerotti, toss briefly and add a tablespoon of grated Parmesan.

9 Serve on warmed plates with extra Parmesan at the table.

Stuffed Shoulder of Welsh Lamb

Undoubtedly Welsh Lamb is the best in the world. It's such a versatile ingredient and in this recipe the punchy flavours of porcini, truffle, lemon and herbs make it really special, whilst the spinach keeps the meat really succulent during the slow roasting.

Ingredients

1.5kg shoulder of Welsh lamb, (with bones removed)

1 teaspoon sea salt

½ level teaspoon black pepper

12 large banana shallots, peeled

1 tablespoon olive oil

Stuffing

30g unsalted butter

100g shallot, chopped very finely

200g spinach

3 fat garlic cloves, finely grated with 1 teaspoon sea salt

200g chestnut mushroom, chopped very finely

30g dried porcini soaked in 5 tablespoons boiling water

1 tablespoon of tartufo (truffle) paste

1 teaspoon lemon zest

1 tablespoon lemon juice

3 sprigs of thyme, leaves only

200g fresh breadcrumbs

1 small free-range egg, beaten

Serves 4-6

What you do

1 First, make the stuffing – melt half of the butter in a large frying pan, add the spinach and wilt, remove and drain on kitchen paper.

2 Add the remaining butter to the pan and add the shallots, stir through and then cook over a medium heat until really soft and golden. Stir in the garlic and cook for a minute, then add the chestnut mushrooms, stir through. Drain the porcini soaking juice into the mushrooms and continue cooking until the moisture has evaporated, this will concentrate the flavour.

3 Chop the porcini and add to the mushrooms. Stir in the tartufo paste followed by the lemon zest, lemon juice and thyme. Cook for a

further 5 minutes and stir in the breadcrumbs.

4 Tip into a mixing bowl and leave to cool. Stir in the egg to combine everything. Stuffing is now ready.

5 To prepare the lamb, open out the de-boned shoulder on your prep board and season well with salt and pepper. Pack the stuffing along the centre of the meat, roll up and secure with string in several places along the joint, tucking in any rough edges at each end.

6 Mix the banana shallots with the olive oil and place in a roasting tin with the lamb. Roast at 220°C/200°C Fan/Gas 7 for 20 minutes, then reduce the heat to 160°C/150°C Fan/Gas 3 for 1 hour. If you prefer your meat well done, cook for a further 20 minutes.

7 Remove the lamb and place on a warm plate with the shallots, cover with foil and rest for 20 minutes.

Quick sauce

1 If you would like to make a quick sauce, spoon off the excess fat from the juices, place the pan over a medium heat and boil, add 1 tablespoon of brandy and 100ml white wine. Stir to dissolve any sticky juices then pour in 200ml of good meat stock. Taste and check the seasoning. Thicken with a dessertspoon of arrowroot dissolved in a little water. Add in a little at a time stirring continuously until thickened slightly and glossy.

2 Slice the lamb into thick slabs and serve with seasonal vegetables.

Beef Bourguignon

This has to be one of my favourite classic dishes. I like big chunks of Welsh beef, good wine and plenty of garlic bread to mop up the juices. The secret of any dish is cooking the ingredients into layers of flavour in order to get the intensity and complexity.

Ingredients

1.2kg Welsh beef e.g. chuck, blade or shin trimmed of sinew and cut into 8 large pieces

2 tablespoons olive or rapeseed oil

4 thick slices streaky bacon, cut into lardons (tiny strips)

16 small round shallots (plunge in boiling water for 5 minutes, drain and remove skins).

50g salted butter

1 garlic clove, grated

200g little button mushrooms

1 bottle of nice red Burgundy, Merlot or Pinot Noir

400ml good beef stock – consommé is really good

1 tablespoon tomato purée

4 sprigs thyme

2 bay leaves

½ teaspoon sea salt

½ teaspoon freshly ground black pepper

To thicken

25g plain flour

25g soft butter

Serves 4-6

What you do

1 Pat the beef dry with kitchen paper. Heat a skillet pan on med-high heat, add the oil and sear the beef pieces in batches of 4 on both sides until brown. Remove and place in a casserole dish.

2 Cook the bacon in the skillet until lightly browned, remove with a slotted spoon and add to the beef.

3 Add the shallots and butter to the skillet, gently colour over a medium heat. Stir in the garlic and then the mushrooms, cook for 2 minutes then remove with a slotted spoon and pop them in with the beef.

④ Deglaze the pan with the wine, bring to a simmer stirring to dissolve any sticky meat residue.

⑤ Add the beef stock, tomato paste, thyme and bay leaf, bubble for 5 minutes then pour over meat in the casserole, add the salt and pepper. Cover and place in the oven for 3 to 3½ hours at 160°C/140°C Fan/Gas 3.

⑥ Remove the beef from the oven, check to make sure it is lovely and tender, taste and season accordingly.

⑦ To thicken, mix together the flour and butter forming a paste. Place the casserole over a low heat so it simmers gently and whisk in the butter and flour paste a third at a time until thickened to your liking. I like to serve this with simple greens or buttered carrots and garlic bread. I also like to serve the same wine with the dish as I used in cooking!

Slow Cooked Italian Meatballs with Gnocchi

Italian courses are so popular at the Cookery School and this is a lovely exercise in mastering 3 classic elements: meatballs, ragù and gnocchi. So take time, relax and enjoy the process.

Ingredients

Meatballs

400g Welsh beef or pork, or both, minced

2 slices mortadella or Parma ham, finely chopped

1 small onion, finely chopped and cooked in olive oil

1 fat garlic clove, finely grated with sea salt

1 tablespoon chopped parsley

75g breadcrumbs

1 teaspoon vegetable powder (Marigold Swiss)

Tomato Ragù

4 tablespoons olive oil

1 large onion, peeled and sliced thinly

1 stick of celery, finely chopped, use the leaves too

2 fat garlic cloves, peeled and finely chopped

1 level teaspoon sea salt

½ teaspoon black pepper

½ teaspoon sugar

400ml passata, or chopped tinned tomatoes

1 teaspoon of tomato purée

200ml vegetable stock (Marigold Swiss)

1 tablespoon chopped herbs, try rosemary, sage, parsley

Good olive oil to finish

Potato Gnocchi

450g starchy potatoes – try Italian Spunta or British Desiree

2 small eggs, lightly beaten

About 200g plain flour – you may not need all of it

1 rounded teaspoon sea salt

½ teaspoon white pepper

¼ teaspoon nutmeg

Serves 4

What you do

Tomato Ragù

1 Heat the olive oil in a large pan. Add the onion and fry until soft and slightly golden, then add the chopped celery and cook for about 5 minutes.

2 Stir in the garlic and cook for a minute, then add the salt, pepper and sugar. Add the tomatoes and stock, bring to the boil, then reduce to a slow simmer and cook for about 30 minutes.

The Meatballs

3 Place all the ingredients in a food processor and pulse to combine everything. Wet your hands with cold water and divide the mixture into 18-24 equal portions and roll them into balls.

4 Heat some oil in a pan and fry the meatballs in batches until golden all over. Drain on kitchen paper, then transfer to the ragù sauce. Cover with a lid and gently simmer in the sauce for 30 minutes, adding a little water if the sauce gets a little dry.

Gnocchi

5 Wash the potatoes, place them in a large saucepan (in their skins) cover with cold water and boil until tender and then drain. While they are still hot, peel off the skins, cut up and push through a potato ricer onto a clean surface. Make a well in the centre; add the eggs, and about ¾ of the flour and the salt. Start to combine to form a soft warm dough.

6 Roll into long thick sausages about 1.25cm/ ½ inch thick. Cut into nugget sizes and mark with a fork. Place on a floured tray. Cook the gnocchi in fast boiling salted water. Drain well and finish with a drizzle of olive oil and some Parmesan, serve with the rich and saucy meatballs.

Roast Carrot
Salad with
Pomegranate

Ingredients

750g small carrots, yellow and purple are delicious too, so mix them up

300g leeks

200g greens: chard, kale, purple sprouting or spinach

2 teaspoons cumin seeds

2 tablespoons maple or agave syrup

2½ tablespoons rose harissa

3 tablespoons olive oil

1 level teaspoon sea salt

About 8 stems coriander, leaves roughly chopped, stems finely chopped

3 tablespoons pomegranate molasses

1 tablespoon maple syrup

2 teaspoons lemon juice

Serves 4

What you do

1 Heat the oven to 220°C/ 200°C Fan/Gas 7.

2 The carrots need to be peeled then cut if they are not small enough. I use "Ladies' Fingers", or okra, as a measure. If the carrots are small, just leave them whole, or cut them lengthways in half or even quarters to get the uniformish size.

3 To make the coating for the carrots, mix together the cumin seeds, maple or agave syrup, harissa paste, olive oil, and the salt. Add the carrots and mix well then tip out onto a parchment-lined baking tin. Roast for 15-20 minutes until the carrots start to get sticky.

4 Meanwhile, prepare the leeks and the greens. Trim the leeks and remove the outer fibrous layers, then shred and wash thoroughly, drain well. Wash the greens and trim the stems, cutting them down if they are thick.

5 Remove the carrots from the oven and mix in the leeks, return to the oven for about 15-20 minutes until the leeks begin to turn golden. Remove from the oven, add the chard, spinach or kale and mix through. Pop back in the oven for a further 10 minutes, make sure the greens are cooked through and slightly wilted. Mix together the pomegranate molasses, maple syrup and lemon juice, pour over the vegetables and mix through. Sprinkle with the chopped coriander and serve.

Serve hot or cold. I love to add chunks of hot succulent roast chicken, crumbled feta or flakes of hot smoked fish. You can also add grains such as freekeh and red rice or beans such as canelinni or borlotti to make a delicious and healthy lunch box.

OMG Chocolate Cake!

Ingredients

100g "Softer" unsalted butter

A little extra butter for greasing and some flour for dusting

140g good quality dark chocolate with around 70% cocoa solids

6 large free-range eggs, separated

140g ground almonds

1 teaspoon Halen Môn vanilla salt

1 tablespoon Amaretto (optional)

85g caster sugar

Ganache

240ml double cream

2 tablespoons caster sugar

2 teaspoons Halen Môn vanilla sea salt

200g good quality dark chocolate, as above

Serves 6-8

What you do

1 Preheat the oven to 170°C/150°C Fan/Gas 3. Grease a 23cm/9in spring-form cake tin and line the base with greaseproof or baking parchment. Dust the sides with a little flour.

To make the cake

2 Put the chocolate and butter into a heatproof bowl set over a pan of gently simmering water. Heat until melted, then remove the bowl from the pan and stir until smooth. Leave for about 5 minutes to cool slightly.

3 Stir in the egg yolks, ground almonds, and the Amaretto, if using. Put the egg whites into a large bowl, add a pinch of salt and whisk until soft peaks form. Continue whisking, adding the sugar a little at a time, until stiff peaks form. Stir 2 tablespoons of the egg whites into the chocolate mixture and mix through thoroughly, this will loosen the mixture so you can then gently fold in the remaining whites.

DON'T OVER MIX!

④ Pour and scrape the mixture into the prepared tin and bake for 30-35 minutes until well risen and just firm to the touch. Cool in the tin, the middle may sink slightly, but this is ok as it will be soft and chocolatey.

To finish, make the ganache

⑤ Chop the chocolate into small pieces and pop into a mixing bowl. Pour the double cream into a saucepan, add the caster sugar and 1 teaspoon of the sea salt, heat until it is almost at boiling point. Take off the heat and pour over the chocolate. Leave for 5 minutes, then stir until the chocolate melts into a silky smooth sauce. Leave to cool, stirring occasionally. As it cools it will thicken up and be easier to control when coating the cake.

⑥ Put the cake on a serving plate or cake stand. Pour the thickened ganache onto the centre of the cake and ease outward and down the sides with a palette knife – don't be in a hurry to do this. Finish with a sprinkle of the remaining vanilla sea salt. Slice and serve with coffee-cream.

Coffee Cream

300ml double cream
1 teaspoon vanilla extract
1 tablespoon icing sugar (sifted)
4 tablespoons espresso coffee.

Whip together until soft creamy peaks form. Perhaps a tablespoon of brandy might be nice.

Serving Suggestion

I used the following to embellish the cake – 1 tablespoon bronze popping candy, 1 heaped tablespoon chopped pistachios and 1 heaped tablespoon thin strips of candied orange zest (using a vegetable peeler, remove the zest from 2 medium oranges, cut into really thin strips. Squeeze the juice from 1 orange into a saucepan and add 2 tablespoons of caster sugar plus the zest. Bring to the boil and cook for 5 minutes, or until the juice reaches a syrupy consistency. Cool completely before using).

Sticky Almond Cake with Roasted Spiced Plums

I grew up with a version of this recipe that my Mum made from her *Cordon Bleu* magazine in the 70s. Then my friend Jane, who runs Clam's Cakes, developed a sticky almond cake, which is so addictive. Here's my version with some yummy plums.

Ingredients

150g unsalted butter

75g caster sugar

90g molasses sugar

4 large eggs

50g wholemeal flour

1 flat teaspoon sea salt (vanilla flavoured is delicious)

120g ground almonds

50g whole almonds, skins on, chopped

100g marzipan, cut into small pieces

Plums

10 plums

2 star anise

1 teaspoon ground cinnamon

1 teaspoon vanilla paste

6 thick strips orange peel

150g caster sugar

Serves 6-8 or 9 mini cakes

What you do

1 First, butter your tart tins, 9 x cupcake size or a single, larger 24cm cake tin. If using a large tin, line the base with a circle of baking parchment. Heat the oven to 180°C/160°C Fan/Gas 4.

2 Cream the butter and sugars together until the mixture becomes lighter in colour and texture. Mix the eggs in, one at a time, followed by the flour, sea salt and ground almonds. Fold in half of the chopped almonds and half the marzipan pieces, spoon into the cake moulds or cake tin. Top with the remaining chopped almonds and marzipan pieces.

3 Bake for 12-15 minutes for small cakes and about 30 minutes for a larger cake. The finished cakes should be pale golden in colour and deliciously soft in the centre.

For the plums

4 Line a baking tin with parchment paper. Cut the plums into quarters and remove the stone. Place in the baking tin so they fit quite tightly. Mix together the spices, orange and vanilla with the sugar and rub together so the sugar picks up some of the essential oils. Sprinkle all over the plums and roast for about 15-20 minutes until the juices start to ooze and form a yummy syrup. Remove the plums from the pan with a slotted spoon on to a serving plate, mix the juices and spices together and then pour over the plums. Sometimes I decorate the top of the cake with the plums and it looks gorgeous!

I love to serve this with strained yoghurt scented with a little orange blossom water and a drizzle of honey.

Pineapple Upside-Down Pudding

This is a more grown-up version from the one my mum use to make. I've dropped the glacé cherries and opted for more tropical mango, sour cherries and a good helping of rum.

Ingredients

1 medium pineapple, trimmed
and peeled

Basting syrup

100ml fresh orange juice

50ml maple syrup

12 cloves for studding

Sticky sauce

25g "Softer" unsalted butter, melted

120g molasses sugar

60ml double cream

1 level teaspoon ground cinnamon

2 tablespoons rum

75g dried mango

40g sour cherries

Batter

240g plain flour

1 teaspoon baking powder

½ teaspoon vanilla sea salt

¼ teaspoon baking soda

160ml low fat yoghurt

2 large free-range eggs

125g "Softer" unsalted butter,

180g golden caster sugar

To finish

2 tablespoons rum

Serves 6-8

What you do

1 Stud the pineapple all over with the cloves. Place in a roasting tin and brush with some of the syrup. Set your oven to 200°C/180°C Fan/Gas 6 and roast the pineapple using the syrup to baste during the cooking time – about 35-40 minutes.

Sticky Sauce

2 Combine the butter, sugar, cream, cinnamon and rum in a saucepan and bring to the boil until the sugar melts and forms a sticky sauce. Pour into a rectangle cake tin or oven dish. Chop the dried mango and scatter into the sauce, add the sour cherries.

The Batter

3 Sift the flour, baking powder, salt, and baking soda into a mixing bowl. In a smaller bowl, whisk together the low fat yoghurt and eggs.

4 Using an electric mixer, cream together the softened butter and sugar until light and fluffy. Lower the speed and whisk in the low fat yoghurt and eggs, followed by the flour mixture. Use a rubber spatula to scrape any ingredients from the sides and beat into the batter mixture until smooth.

5 Remove the pineapple from the oven and remove the cloves. Slice into 8 rounds and lay on top of the sticky sauce. Pour the batter mixture over the top and smooth to the edges.

6 Bake in a preheated oven at 180°C/160°C Fan/Gas 4 for 50 minutes-1 hour.

To finish

7 Heat the 2 tablespoons of rum, pour over the cake and ignite for an entrance!

8 Serve with vanilla, lime and rum cream (whip together 300ml double cream whipped with 40g icing sugar, 1 flat teaspoon vanilla sea salt, 2 tablespoons lime juice and 1 tablespoon rum).

Little Choux Hearts
filled with Passion
Fruit Cream and
finished with an
Orange Glaze

A little romantic touch for Valentine's Day, why not bake for the love of your life?

Ingredients

Choux Pastry

150g plain flour

1 teaspoon sugar

1 teaspoon salt

100g "Softer" unsalted butter

250ml water

4 eggs

Makes 8

....

What you do

1 Sieve the flour, salt and sugar together twice onto a sheet of parchment.

2 Heat the water and butter together in a pan. When the butter has melted, turn up the heat and bring to a rolling boil. Shoot the flour into the pan as quickly as you can and stir and whip it all together to form a paste that leaves the sides of the pan, forming a glossy ball.

Remove from the heat and keep whipping with a wooden spoon or spatula so that it cools slightly (you can do this with an electric whisk). Beat the eggs together and gradually whisk into the paste. The paste should look glossy but hold its shape on the end of the spoon – remember, you have to push this through a piping nozzle.

3 Preheat the oven to 200°C/180°C Fan/Gas 6.

4 Brush 2 baking sheets with a little melted butter or use parchment paper.

5 Fill a piping bag fitted with a plain nozzle and pipe 8 nice heart shapes, leaving ample space between them to expand.

6 Bake for 15-20 minutes until puffed, golden and really firm to the touch – don't be too hasty to take them out, if they are not fully formed and firmly baked, they will collapse and you'll have flat hearts and you don't want that!

7 When they are baked, quickly pull the trays out and make a slit in the side of each heart so that the steam can escape and they can dry out. Pop them back in the oven, turn the temperature down to 150°C/130°C Fan/Gas 2, and continue cooking for about 15 minutes until they have dried out on the inside. Remove and cool on a rack. Once cooled completely, they will be ready to fill. I would do this just before serving so the choux is crisp.

Passion Fruit Cream Filling

300ml double cream

1 teaspoon vanilla extract

2 tablespoons icing sugar, sifted

200ml crème fraîche

200ml passion fruit pulp or juice (you can use lemon curd too, but only 100ml as it is sweeter)

1 Whisk the double cream together with the vanilla and sugar until soft peaks form – DON"T OVER WHISK! It's better to stop short and finish manually.

2 Fold in the crème fraîche and passion fruit

Orange Icing

300g icing sugar

The zest of a small orange

3 oranges, juiced to form a pouring consistency.

1 Simply sift the icing sugar into the bowl, stir in the orange zest. Gradually stir in enough juice to give a pouring consistency.

Panna cotta
with Jaggery
and Rum
Fruits

All I can say is, wow! I just love this dessert, the jaggery gives the panna cotta a delicious fudgy flavour and the rum fruits are a perfect match.

Ingredients

2 x 2g leaves of gelatine

300ml double cream

115g jaggery, grated

100ml full-fat milk

50ml buttermilk

Vegetable oil, to grease the moulds

Rum syrup

100ml maple syrup

200ml dark rum

1 cinnamon stick

1 star anise

2 cloves

100ml fresh orange juice plus 1 thick piece of zest

1 teaspoon lime grated zest

4 tablespoons lime juice

$^1/_3$ of a small pineapple, chopped finely

Fruit

1 tablespoon dried cranberries

$^2/_3$ of a small pineapple

1 large orange, segmented

Makes 4-6

What you do

Panna cotta

1 First, make the panna cotta. Soak the gelatine leaves in cold water to soften, this will take just a few minutes. Next warm the cream, add the jaggery and stir until dissolved. Remove from the heat. Pick out the gelatine and squeeze the excess water away, add to the hot cream and stir through until melted.

2 Stir in the milk and buttermilk and the mixture is ready. Lightly oil 4 pudding moulds or ramekins, pour in the panna cotta mixture and put them on a baking tray, cover with clingfilm and put in the fridge for 4 hours or overnight to set.

To make the rum fruits

3 First, prepare the syrup. Place everything in a saucepan and bring to the boil, reduce the liquid by half and then strain through a fine sieve into another pan. Bring the syrup to the boil again and cook until it is thickened, it will need to reduce by half again to achieve this. Add the cranberries and cook for a couple of minutes.

4 Trim the pineapple, slice into thin rings, remove the core then cut each ring into little triangle segments and add to the warm syrup. Cut each segment of orange into 3 pieces and add to the syrup. Pour into a bowl, cover and chill.

To serve

5 Briefly dip each panna cotta in hot water to loosen and turn out onto a serving plate. Spoon the fruit and syrup around the panna cotta creating a collar effect and serve.

French Apple Tart with Cider

Another little masterclass in perfecting pastry, forming a tart, baking blind, creating a delicious fruit purée, topping with a classic design and glazing it to produce a perfect dessert.

Ingredients

Pastry

80g unsalted butter

50g caster sugar

1 medium free-range egg yolk

½ teaspoon vanilla salt

175g plain flour

Apple Purée

200ml cider, we love Gwynt –y-Ddraig Orchard Gold medium cider

1 tablespoon calvados or brandy

175g caster sugar

900g cooking apples such as Bramley, peeled and cored

Topping

3-4 sweet eating apples e.g. Golden Delicious

2 tablespoons lemon juice

3 tablespoons apple or quince Jelly or Apricot jam

Serves 6-8

What you do

1 Preheat oven to 200°C /180°C Fan/Gas 6.

2 For the pastry, beat together the butter and sugar until lighter in colour and texture. Stir in the egg, the salt and then sift in the flour, fold in with a spatula and then as it comes together push into a ball with your hand, add a couple of tablespoons of cold water. The dough should be smooth not cracked. Flatten the dough and wrap in clingfilm, chill for 20 minutes.

Apple purée

3 Pour the cider and brandy into a pan, add the sugar and bring to the boil and reduce the liquid by half. Chop the cooking apples and add to the pan, cover and simmer for about 20 minutes until the apple collapses, whip with a spatula to form a purée, set aside to cool.

Making the Tart

④ Roll out pastry, and use it to line a 25cm (10in) loose-bottomed flan tin. Prick the pastry and top with a sheet of baking parchment, $^1/_3$ fill with dried beans or rice and bake blind in the preheated oven for 12 minutes. Remove rice and parchment, and return to oven for another 5 minutes. Reduce the oven heat to 180°C/160°C Fan/Gas 4.

For the top

⑤ Quarter the eating apples, remove the core and thinly slice, toss with the lemon juice. Starting at the edge of the tart, overlap the slices round and round until you end up in the middle creating a nice concentric design. Bake for 30 minutes.

To finish

⑥ Melt the jelly or jam (sieve the jam before brushing so it's really smooth), brush the apples liberally with the jam – your tart is now ready to eat!

Seasonal ingredients

December

Goose, Turkey, Mallard, Hare, Venison, Duck, Guinea Fowl, Grouse, Wood Pigeon, Rabbit, Partridge, Pheasant.

Brill, Clams, Squid, Haddock, Halibut, Hake, John Dory, Lemon Sole, Sea Bass, Trout, Oysters, Scallops, Mussels.

Squash, Brussel Sprouts, Chicory, Red Cabbage, Leeks, Jerusalem Artichokes, Onions, Marrow, Potatoes, Parsnips, Sea Kale, Winter Radishes, Salsify, Celeriac, Turnips, Chestnuts, Quince, Satsumas, Tangerines, Pomegranates.

Special celebrations

Advent Sunday, Christmas Day, Boxing Day, Hogmanay, New Years Eve.

January

Partridge, Hare, Pheasant, Venison, Duck, Guinea Fowl.

Scallops, Brill, Clams, Cockles, Haddock, Halibut, Hake, John Dory, Lemon Sole, Oysters, Mussels, Turbot.

Brussel Sprouts, Celery, Kale, Leeks, Chicory, Swede, Potatoes, Cabbage, Parsnips, Cauliflower, Celeriac, Shallots, Jerusalem Artichokes, Forced Rhubarb, Satsumas, Pomegranates, Clementines, Blood Oranges, Seville Oranges, Walnuts.

Special celebrations

Burns Night, Chinese New Year.

February

Venison, Hare.

Oysters, Hake, John Dory, Brill, Clams, Turbot, Salmon, Mussels, Cockles.

Cabbage, Red Chicory, Kale, Leeks, Brussel Sprouts, Endive, Swede, Onions, Purple Sprouting Broccoli, Parsnips, Walnuts, Medjool Dates, Turnips, Jerusalem Artichokes, Chard, Beetroot, Pears, Pomegranates, Forced Rhubarb, Pineapple, Pomegranates.

Special celebrations

St Valentine's Day, Shrove Tuesday, Ash Wednesday (the beginning of Lent).

Angela Gray's

Cookery School

at Llanerch Vineyard

The Cookery School

It was in the winter of 2010 when I came to meet the Davies family at Llanerch Vineyard with the whole estate under snow. They had just taken on the project of a lifetime, with their son Ryan assuming the tough task of not only bringing everything back to life there (it had been in mothballs for 2 years and was in poor shape), but to build the business into the success it has become. This was some undertaking and I have the deepest respect and admiration for all that has been achieved. Llanerch now has a productive vineyard producing a range of still and sparkling wines under the Cariad label. They also have a lovely boutique style hotel, a great bistro and restaurant, two fabulous event venues and stunning woodland walks. It is the perfect setting for our Cookery School.

I was invited to open a Cookery School at the estate and immediately set to work on my vision and, with their blessing, I developed a range of classes and events I thought would attract people's attention.

My first idea was to set up a cookery demonstration morning (Saturday Morning Kitchen) where I would cook up a plethora of seasonal ingredients into a range of dishes. I hoped that this would attract people to the School to see the lovely space that had been created and the idyllic setting of the Vineyard.

I am pleased to say that people did come and we were packed to the hilt! This event formed the next idea, to create a monthly Lunch Club. The format would be the same, but we would serve a lovely lunch, replicating some of the recipes

demonstrated. Both of these events have now become two of the hottest tickets in the School Calendar.

The School schedule naturally follows the seasons, bringing that sense of change throughout the year, but the class formats remain the same in building skills and culinary confidence. Today we offer a mix of short Skill Builder Classes, themed One Day Courses and a series of Masterclasses, with our customers taking home everything they make to share with friends and family. We also have our regular "Live" events, Pop-Up Restaurants and host an enormous number of corporate days and private events.

During the winter months, I find that our recipes naturally warm up in colour and flavour; there is more depth and richness. This is reflected in the classes we run, from classic Italian and French to spicy

Moroccan and regional Indian. The festive season also takes precedence in our schedule, with lots of themed classes designed to help people get ahead with dishes they can make, freeze and preserve. We also hold our annual "Stir Up Sunday" event where we each make a Christmas cake, pudding and mince pies, it's such a lovely atmosphere and we all feel a little Christmassy!

Our busy year ends with a real highlight for us, our "Festive Kitchen" events. They are non-stop cooking, drinking, sampling and feasting, featuring a rich mix of ideas, tips and recipes designed to wow friends and family over the Christmas and New Year Holidays. There are delicious home-baked treats and gifts to buy, plus we pull all the stops out to produce a celebratory lunch. These events provide a fitting and wonderful end to our busy year.

Into the New Year we find ourselves at full pelt with classes booked to the maximum with people who have been treated to one of our vouchers for Christmas to attend a culinary experience with us. We start to focus on dishes that will invigorate the palette and digestion after weeks of indulgence. Marinades, spices and different pastes are used to enliven every day dishes from a simple soup to a delicious barbecued chicken – yes, we do barbecue all year round and it's terrific fun!

As we approach March, we have a lot to look forward during the spring months, with lighter and brighter colours and flavours. I look forward to sharing some more seasonal inspiration with you in the next collection of my recipes.

About Angela Gray

Angela has worked prolifically in the food world, starting her career as a personal chef working in Europe and North America. Her clients included an esteemed list, from European aristocracy to high profile clients such as Lord Lloyd Webber. Angela then moved into the restaurant business where she developed her relaxed style of cuisine with a strong Mediterranean influence.

She later returned home to Wales where her culinary path changed direction and led her to university where she studied for 3 years and gained a BSc Honours degree in food science. Whilst studying, Angela also ran a small catering business and held a twice-monthly Cooking Club in her home. This would later form the basis of the television cookery series that was to come her way.

Angela was talent spotted after producer Mark John (Vision Thing), read some of her articles in a magazine. Next came two prime time cookery series for BBC Wales, *Hot Stuff* and *More Hot Stuff*. She also has several radio series to her credit including *My Life on a Plate* and *Packed Lunch*. Angela remains a consistent contributor in the media world.

Her Cookery School opened in 2011 and was cited in *The Independent* and *The Telegraph* as one of the top ten UK Cookery Schools. Together with her team, she has entertained people from all over the world and has created a popular venue and experience for corporate team building and private events. She is a mentor to young budding culinary talent and is most at home when sharing her passion for great cooking. In her own words "it's a dream job!"

Thank you

To all my teachers in life – Mum first – you are always at my side.

To my family, we are all food lovers, so it is always a pleasure to be together and share a feast. Olivia, you have been my inspiration and reason for pushing forward in life.

To Mr Gray our laundry man, DIY man, gardener and general gofer – your cheque is in the post!

To Peter Andrews for introducing me to the Davies family.

To Ryan, Gwyn and Janine for their support over the years.

To my team, Sarah and Pam, you have been with me the longest, you are so amazing and supportive.

To Peter Gill for the opportunity to do this series of books – bless you!

To André for interpreting my recipes for the photo shoot.

To Huw for colouring the book with beautiful photographs and helping me include some special family history with props collected from 5 generations. You're a true artist!

To Ross, our young bundle of talent who came to lend a hand during the shoot – you have an exciting career ahead of you!

To all the people who have made the School a success – it's all for you!

People we love

Halen Môn
www.halenmon.com

Gwynt-Y-Ddraig Cider
www.gwyntcidershop.com

Welsh Lamb and Beef
(Hybu Cig Cymru-HCC)
www.eatwelshlambandwelshbeef.com

Pork Wales (Porc Wales)
porc.wales

Castle Dairies (Welsh Butter and The Softer Butter Company)
www.facebook.com/softerbutterco

'During the winter months, I find that our recipes naturally warm up in colour and flavour; there is more depth and richness.'